HOLT McDOUGAL

APA and ASA Writing Guide

HOLT McDOUGAL
a division of Houghton Mifflin Harcourt

Contents

The *APA and ASA Writing Guide* provides students with different tools that will help them become better writers. Designed to support Holt McDougal's *Psychology: Principles in Practice* and *Sociology: the Study of Human Relationships*, the book guides students through the stages of the writing process to produce a research paper.

The book consists of two parts. Part 1: APA Writing Guide will help your students produce a research paper that meets the style guidelines of the American Psychological Association. Part 2: ASA Writing Guide can be used to help students draft a research paper that meets the style guidelines set forth by the American Sociological Association.

Both the APA and the ASA writing guides are structured to provide students with guidelines and resources that guide them through the stages of the writing process:

- **Prewriting** This section provides students with information and worksheets that will help them make a plan for writing; choose a topic; write a thesis statement; and research, gather, and organize information.

- **Writing** The writing section includes guidelines and worksheets designed to help students organize their ideas, write a first draft, develop paragraphs, learn and practice APA or ASA style, and create a reference list.

- **Revising** In this section, students will find strategies for evaluating and revising their paper, along with a checklist for finalizing a research paper, a peer evaluation form, and a self evaluation form.

- **Publishing** The resources in the publishing section lead students through the final steps of the writing process—proofreading, publishing, and reflecting on their work. The chart of "Proofreading Symbols" included in this section will help students evaluate their own work, as well as the work of their peers.

Lastly, additional resources at the back of this book will help your students become more efficient researchers and writers. For example, the "Wordy Phrases" list provides suggestions for alternative phrasing that will enhance the clarity of your students' writing. The "Electronic Resources Glossary" has been included to help your students grasp the variety of electronic resources now available to them.

Holt McDougal Social Studies' *APA and ASA Writing Guide* has been designed to help you refine your writing skills and guide you step-by-step through the writing process for a social studies research report or paper. For an overview of the writing process, see the "Your Writing Process" chart on the following page.

This writing guide will also introduce you to two common social science style guides: the *Publication Manual of the American Psychological Association* (APA) and the *ASA Style Guide*, published by the American Sociological Association. Respectively, these style guides provide guidelines for authors of psychology or sociology papers and reports.

This book is divided into two main parts. Part 1: APA Writing Guide supports psychology students using Holt McDougal's *Psychology: Principles in Practice*. Part 2: ASA Writing Guide is for sociology students using Holt McDougal's *Sociology: the Study of Human Relationships*.

Each part of this writing guide will walk you through the stages of the writing process:

- **Prewriting**
- **Writing**
- **Revising**
- **Publishing**

At each stage, guidelines and strategies have been provided to help you improve specific writing skills. These skills include selecting a writing topic; writing a thesis; making source and note cards; writing a first draft using either APA or ASA styles; and skills for revising, proofreading, and publishing your work. For both parts of this book, eleven worksheets have been provided to reinforce these skills and to help you prepare either a psychology or sociology research paper.

At the back of this book are additional resources that will help you become a more effective social studies writer. The "Wordy Phrases" list provides suggestions for alternative phrasing that will help you express yourself in a straightforward and clear way. Lastly, the "Electronic Resources Glossary" has been included to help you better understand the variety of electronic resources now available for writers.

PREWRITING

- Set **goals** and choose a manageable **topic**.
- Identify your **purpose and audience**.
- Draft a thesis sentence that expresses your **main idea**.
- **Gather information** about the topic.
- Begin to **organize** the information.

WRITING

- Draft an **introduction** that gets your reader's attention and states your main idea.
- Provide **background information**.
- Follow a **plan** for organizing your ideas.
- State your **supporting points** and **elaborate** on them.
- Wrap things up with a **conclusion**.

REVISING

- **Evaluate** your draft, or ask a peer to evaluate it.
- **Revise the draft** to improve its content, organization, and style.

PUBLISHING

- **Proofread** your draft to find and correct spelling, punctuation, and grammar errors.
- **Use** correct manuscript **style**.
- **Publish** your writing.
- **Reflect** on your writing experience.

Part 1: APA Writing Guide

THE PREWRITING STAGE The prewriting stage is where you identify your purpose and audience, decide what to write about, draw upon what you know about the topic, and plan. The guidelines and worksheets that follow for setting goals and limits, choosing a topic, and gathering information will help you as you plan your paper.

Setting Goals and Limits

Before you begin a trip, you must know your destination—where you want to go. You must also consider the travel options that are available and the limits, such as time and money, you have for the trip. Likewise, before you begin the process of writing a paper, you must determine not only what you want the paper to achieve but what is possible given the assignment schedule and available resources. Set your goals and determine the limits of your paper by considering the points that follow.

- **Understand the final product.** Make sure that you understand the exact form and requirements of your research paper. How long should your paper be? Should it be typed or handwritten? What elements— title page, abstract, reference list, and so forth—must be included?

- **Create a project time line for your paper.** Count the days between the day you can begin working on the paper and the date it is due. Set up a time line that shows the date by which you will complete each stage of the writing process.

- **Determine the purpose of your paper.** The purpose of your paper will influence how you select, include, and present information. A paper can have more than one purpose—to inform and to persuade, for example. Other examples of purpose are to compare and contrast, to take a stand and defend it, and to explain or describe. Even though your main purpose is to inform, you may also have a secondary purpose—to compare and contrast, to explain a causal relationship, or to analyze data that you have collected. If the assignment does not specify the purpose of the paper, you must do so.

- **Identify your audience.** Who is your likely audience? If readers do not already know something about your topic, you will need to provide background information.

- **Think about how you will be evaluated.** Ask your teacher for a description of the criteria that will be used to evaluate your paper. List the criteria point by point. To the list, add the personal goals and standards that you want your paper to achieve. Use the final list to create an evaluation checklist that you can refer to as you develop your paper.

Choosing a Topic

Try to write about something that interests you. If you have been assigned a topic that holds little appeal for you, perhaps you can find an interesting aspect of it on which to concentrate.

Even if you have already chosen or been assigned a broad topic, you should take time to refine it to match your goals and suit your audience within the space and time limits of the assigned paper. Narrowing your topic before you begin will simplify and hasten the research process.

IDEAS AND CONTENT

- **Explore ideas and choose a topic.** Ask questions. Try finding a topic by asking questions about subjects that interest you.

- **Gather ideas and details to develop the topic.** Look at good sources of information, such as books, magazines, encyclopedias, the Internet, and experts in your community. Then provide logical support for your ideas by using facts, examples, statistics, and expert opinions.

- **Think about your audience and your purpose for writing.** Ask "Who am I writing for?" "What do my readers need to know?" "What will they find interesting?" "Why am I writing this paper?"

ORGANIZATION

- **Develop a thesis or controlling idea.** Narrow your topic so that it is not too big. For example, the topic of "the three most important schools of psychology" is too big. An explanation of Sigmund Freud's idea of repression is too narrow. You need something in between, such as how Freud's ideas about defense mechanisms contributed to the field of psychology.

- **Organize the ideas and details into a coherent structure.** Try using order of importance. Start with your least important idea and save the most important idea for last. That way, the reader will better remember your most important ideas.

VOICE

- **Think about your topic—what voice should you use?** Your tone (friendly, calm, stern, neutral) should match your purpose and your topic. For example, a paper about the causes and effects of violence needs to be formal, and serious.

APA Writing Guide

Choosing a Topic

Use the graphic organizer and questions below to help you choose a topic, plan research questions, and find sources.

- Choose and narrow a topic that can be researched and will provide information to your reader.
- Answer the questions below to help you organize your thoughts and begin your research.

CHOOSE AND NARROW A RESEARCH TOPIC

Broad topic	
Narrower topic	
Limited topic	

ANSWER QUESTIONS FOR RESEARCH

1. What do I already know about my topic?_____

_____

_____

2. What will my audience want to know about my topic? _____

_____

_____

3. What about my topic interests me? _____

_____

_____

4. What do I need to know about my topic?_____

_____

_____

Writing a Thesis Statement

A thesis statement is a sentence or two identifying the main idea that you intend to explain or prove in your paper. Taking the following steps will help you identify your thesis.

REFRESH YOUR MEMORY

Pick a topic. Then read through your notes and skim your resources to refresh your memory of the information you have.

ASK QUESTIONS

Think about what you now know about the topic. Ask yourself questions about the topic that might lead you to your thesis. Don't try too hard at this point. Just explore the topic and allow questions to occur naturally.

EVALUATE YOUR QUESTIONS

Consider your questions one at a time for thesis potential. For example, suppose you were assigned the broad topic "the psychology of memory." You might come up with the following questions:

- **Question A** Why do many elderly people who have difficulty remembering recent events clearly recall events of years long past?

- **Question B** Why do so many people seek out products that claim to improve memory?

- **Question C** Can memory be improved?

- **Question D** What is the most effective method for improving memory?

- **Question E** Do memory-improvement techniques have lasting effects?

Because **Question A** seems to deal mostly with the physiology of memory, it does not fit a psychology assignment very well. You may discard this question as a basis for your thesis statement.

At first glance, **Question B** seems unrelated to the assignment. As you think the question through, however, you realize that it implies a consumer demand for memory-improvement products. A new question comes to mind—Why do so many people seek out products that claim to improve memory? This question has thesis potential; you set it aside for now.

Several studies have concluded that memory can be improved, so a paper that answers **Question C** may not provide new information or a fresh viewpoint. Still, evaluating your questions leads you to **Question D** and **Question E**, both of which have thesis potential. You now have three questions that might serve as the basis of your thesis. Choose the question that interests you most.

ANSWER YOUR QUESTION

Suppose you chose the following question: Why do so many people seek out products that claim to improve memory? Think of possible answers to your question, such as the following: People want to improve their memory because they associate losing their memory with losing control. People think memory loss is inevitable as they age. People want to improve their memory because good memory is considered a sign of youth and good health. People fear their memory may not be as good as the memory of other people their age. People do not accurately judge the reliability of their own memory. Now identify relationships among your answers. For this set of answers you might identify the following points:

- People set great value on having a reliable memory.
- People fear personal memory loss.
- People expect memory loss as they age.
- People are not able to accurately evaluate their own memory.

WRITE AND REFINE YOUR THESIS

Again, the thesis statement gives the main point of the paper. Consider the points you have come up with. Choose one or combine two or more of these points to formulate a rough thesis statement. For example: The fear of memory loss causes people great stress.

To be effective, a thesis statement must meet the following criteria:

- answer a relevant question that could be asked about the topic,
- contain qualifiers that limit the statement to a precise and defensible point,
- be an affirmative statement, and
- be as brief as possible (one sentence is ideal).

Apply these criteria to the rough thesis statement above. The first criterion is met because the rough thesis statement would answer the question "Does fear of memory loss cause people serious stress?" The next criterion is not met because, as the statement now reads, the implication is that all people are always experiencing stress because of their fear of memory loss. This obviously is not true. Looking back at the list of main points that you developed from answering your question, you are reminded that people expect memory loss as they age.

You could refine the rough thesis statement to read: "For most people, fear of memory loss becomes an increasing cause of serious stress as they age." Continuing with your evaluation, you see the thesis statement is now limited, is affirmative, and is brief. In short, it meets all of the remaining criteria. You may revise your thesis statement as you work on your paper, but for now use what you settle on as your guide. Worksheet 2 provides practice in writing thesis statements.

APA Writing Guide

Prewriting

Writing a Thesis Statement

Use the graphic organizer and questions below to write and refine a thesis statement based on your topic.

- Brainstorm a list of potential research questions about your topic and evaluate your questions for thesis potential.
- Select a research question to answer and write a thesis statement

ASK QUESTIONS ABOUT YOUR TOPIC

Questions	Thesis Potential
Question 1:	___ Yes ___ No
Question 2:	___ Yes ___ No
Question 3:	___ Yes ___ No
Question 4:	___ Yes ___ No
Question 5:	___ Yes ___ No

WRITE A THESIS STATEMENT

My research question:	
Answer to my research question:	
My thesis statement:	

Gathering and Organizing Information

You will save yourself a great deal of time if you do some preliminary planning before beginning the information-gathering part of your research. You have already chosen a topic that arouses your curiosity, one about which you have questions. These questions can give your research some direction. You might want to brainstorm or use the *5W-How?* questions (who, what, when, where, why, and how) to help define your topic and clarify how best to proceed with research. For example, the questions below could help guide research on why people buy products that claim to improve memory.

- **Who** buys products that claim to improve memory?
- **What** techniques can be used to improve memory?
- **When** is memory loss most likely to occur during the aging process?
- **Where** is the capacity for memory located in the brain?
- **Why** do so many people fear memory loss?
- **How** can memory loss be prevented or repaired?

FINDING SOURCES OF INFORMATION

Begin your research with a general look at, or overview of, your topic. Try one or a combination of the following sources to construct an overview. Not only will you find valuable background information, but you may also get leads on additional sources.

- In encyclopedias or other general reference books, read one or two articles about your topic, or if the topic is highly limited, about related topics. For example, you would not find an article explaining why people purchase products to improve their memory. You would, however, find articles on memory and memory loss, both of which are general topics.

- Search the Internet for information about your topic. Besides providing information you might use, a Web site might provide links to other useful sites.

- Interview an expert (a teacher, professor, librarian, parent, or neighbor) on your topic. Such a person might be able to direct you to research materials that would prove extremely useful.

Once you have an adequate overview of your topic, you are ready to look for specific sources of information. All sources can be classified as either primary or secondary. A **primary source** provides firsthand, original information. It may be a letter, speech, research report, eyewitness account, personal remembrance, or autobiography. A **secondary source** contains secondhand, or indirect, information. An encyclopedia, an expert's

opinion, a magazine article, and a biography are all secondary sources—
someone's interpretation, analysis, or opinion of primary sources. Because
each type has its advantages, good researchers draw information from both
sources. Primary sources present you with original material that you can
interpret for yourself. Secondary sources present you with the perspectives
of others who have studied your topic. Of course, in your search for
information, you will want to explore both print and nonprint sources.

Sources of Information	
Library Resources	
Source	**What to Look for**
Card catalog or online catalog	Books, records, audiotapes, and videotapes (print and audiovisual listings are in separate catalogs in some libraries)
Online periodical indexes	Magazine and journal articles, indexed by subject and author
Indexes to newspapers, essays and articles	Articles from major newspapers, such as *The New York Times*; possible local newspapers (newspapers are frequently archived online or on microfilm)
Specialized reference books and CD-ROMs	Encyclopedias of special subjects, such as almanacs and biographical references
Online databases, microfilm, or microfiche	Indexes to major newspapers; back issues of many major newspapers and magazines
Community Resources	
Source	**What to Look for**
Internet and online services	Articles, interviews, bibliographies, pictures, videos, and sound recordings
Museums, historical societies, professional organizations, and government offices	Exhibits, records, and experts
Schools and colleges	Libraries, experts, exhibits, special collections, and records
Television and radio, videostores	Documentary and instructional programs and videos.

EVALUATE YOUR SOURCES

Because so many sources are available, you may have difficulty knowing which ones to use to evaluate the sources you find. Apply the *4R* test.

- **Relevant?** The source must contain information directly related to your topic.

- **Recent?** Always use sources that are as current as possible. Even in a slow-changing field of psychology, you should read the most recent publications. They will often show you, in their bibliographies, which older sources of information are still important.

- **Reliable?** The source must be accurate. Generally, a respected scholar or a respected newspaper or journal, such as *The Washington Post* or *Psychology Today*, will provide trustworthy information. If in doubt about a source, consult a librarian or expert.

- **Representative?** If your topic is controversial, find sources with information and opinions supporting both sides, even if you draw a conclusion that one side's position is stronger.

ORGANIZE YOUR SOURCES

Just as you have consulted references cited in secondary works, readers of your research paper may want to consult your sources for additional information on your topic. In a References list at the end of your paper, you will need to provide precise details about every source you have used. For this reason, always carefully record information about sources as you use them. Otherwise, you may find yourself running back to the library or making a hasty, last-minute phone call to track down source information.

   Use the suggestions below to help you record your sources. Completing Worksheet 3 will help you learn the correct style for noting sources.

- **Make a source card or bibliography card for every source you use.** You may keep your list on index cards, in a computer file, or simply on several pages of a notebook.

- **Number your sources. Assign each source a number.** Then you can write the number, rather than author and title, when you are taking notes from a given source.

- **Record all publishing information.** Take down everything you might need for your References list, such as title and subtitle, an editor or translator, volume number, city, publisher, original publication date, and revised edition date.

- **Note the call number or the location of the source.** This information will save you time if you must go back to a source later.

RESEARCH AND TAKE NOTES

Now you are ready to leap into a major phase of your research project—the search for specific information. As you examine your source material, you will take notes on the facts, examples, and opinions pertinent to your topic. There are three ways to record this information: **summarizing**, **paraphrasing**, and **quoting directly**.

Note-Taking Strategies	
Strategy	**Use**
A **summary** is a brief restatement of main ideas and important details.	To note general ideas about your topic that do not require detailed discussion, such as an alternative viewpoint
A **paraphrase** is a restatement that retains more details than a summary and is about the same length as the original.	To include pertinent details, such as names, dates, and statistics
A **direct quotation** is the exact words of an author or speaker and is always enclosed in quotation marks.	To note ideas that are especially well phrased, to be sure of technical accuracy, and to refer to passages from works of literature

CREATE NOTE CARDS

Use the guidelines below for creating note cards. Completing Worksheet 3 will help you learn the correct style for taking notes.

- **Use a separate note card, sheet of paper, or computer file for each source and for each main idea.** Having separate records for each source and each main idea will make sorting and grouping your notes easier.

- **Write the source number in the upper right-hand corner and the page number(s) at the bottom of the note card.** Both numbers are essential for correct documentation. The source number gives you access to the publication data on your corresponding source card. The page numbers must be supplied if you use the information in your paper.

- **Write a label at the top of the card showing the main idea.** The labels will let you see content at a glance and are useful in preparing your working outline.

- **Re-read the note to make sure you understand it.** Decipher any abbreviations or note-taking shortcuts that might be unclear when you are writing your paper.

Making Source Cards and Note Cards

Use graphic organizers like the ones below to record sources and take
notes.

- Make a source card for each of your sources.

- Complete your note cards. Make sure to record quotes accurately, give
  credit to authors, and paraphrase by completely rewriting ideas.

SAMPLE SOURCE CARD

Source number: _____
Publishing information:
Annotation:
Call number:

SAMPLE NOTE CARD

Source number: _____
Heading (the main idea):
Note (direct quotation, paraphrase, or summary):
Page number: _____

THE WRITING STAGE In the writing stage you express your main ideas clearly, support those ideas, and follow a plan of organization, adjusting the plan as needed to make meaning clear. The guidelines that follow and Worksheet 4 will help you as you write your first draft.

Organizing Information

With your topic clearly defined and your thesis statement as a guide, you are now ready to organize the mass of information that you have collected. Every essay or paper has three parts: an introduction that usually states the thesis, a body that presents at least two supporting points, and a conclusion that summarizes and supports the main point.

If you have labeled notes by main idea, you can sort your notes into groups by main idea. You can set aside notes that aren't useful, and then arrange and rearrange the ones you plan to use until you have identified an organizational pattern for your paper. The chart below provides definitions and examples of some organizational patterns.

Types of Organizational Patterns in Writing		
Pattern	**When Writers Use It**	**How It Works**
Chronological	• to tell a story or relate an event or experience • to explain a process • to show cause and effect	• presents events in the order they occur • shows how things change over time
Spatial	• to describe individual features • to create a complete visual picture	• arranges details by location in space—for example, top to bottom, left to right, clockwise, or near to far
Order of Importance	• to inform • to persuade	• arranges ideas and details from most important to least or vice versa • places emphasis where writer thinks it is most effective
Logical	• to inform or to persuade, often by classifying: defining, dividing a subject into parts, or comparing and contrasting	• groups ideas or details together in ways that illustrate the relationships between them

MAPPING INFORMATION

Organizing your notes and identifying an organizational pattern for your paper paves the way for your outline. An **informal outline**, which allows you to organize main ideas and supporting details without arranging them into outline form with numbers and letters, may be all that you need. Strategies for creating informal outlines include **clustering** and **mapping**. The figure below shows an example of clustering.

Sample Cluster Map: Memory Loss and Aging

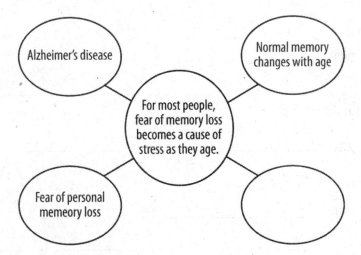

OUTLINING INFORMATION

Your teacher may also require that you turn in a final, formal outline to serve as a table of contents for your final paper. This outline must follow standard outline format as shown in the sample of a partial outline below. Completing Worksheet 4 will help you organize your notes in outline form.

Sample Outline: Memory Loss and Aging

   I. Introduction

  II. Biological Changes

     A. Symptoms

     B. Causes

        1. Normal Aging

        2. Alzheimer's Disease

 III. Research

     A. Prevention

     B. Memory Improvement

 IV. Conclusion

Preparing an Outline

Complete the graphic organizer below, and use it to help you write your
first draft. Include a list of your sources. Use additional paper if necessary.

TOPIC: _____

OUTLINE
I. Introduction

  A. Thesis statement:

   _____

  B. Background information:

   _____

II. Body

  A. First main point: _____

    1. Evidence: _____

      a. _____

      b. _____

    2. Evidence: _____

      a. _____

      b. _____

  B. Second main point: _____

    1. Evidence: _____

      a. _____

      b. _____

    2. Evidence: _____

      a. _____

      b. _____

C. Third main point: _____

   1. Evidence: _____

      a. _____

      b. _____

   2. Evidence: _____

      a. _____

      b. _____

III. Conclusion

A. Restatement of thesis:

_____

B. Closing thought:

_____

SOURCES

1.	
2.	
3.	
4.	

Drafting the Paper

Before you begin writing, gather all of your notes, your outline, and any other materials. Then, use the framework for writing below along with the guidelines for developing paragraphs that follow and Worksheet 5 to write your first draft.

Writing a Research Paper	
Framework	**Directions and Explanations**
Introduction: • Hook your readers. • Provide necessary background. • Include your thesis statement.	• **Use a title page and formal outline if appropriate.** Follow your teacher's instructions. • **Grab your readers' attention right away.** Use a vivid scene, interesting detail, or striking quotation. • **Include background information.** Provide readers with enough background about your topic to make your paper understandable. • **State your thesis.** Clearly state your main idea about your research; incorporate it smoothly into the introduction.
Body: • Develop the first idea that supports your thesis. • Develop the second idea and so on.	• **Present your research.** Be certain that you support each major point about your thesis with evidence from a variety of sources. Be sure to cite your sources, and distinguish your own ideas from those of your sources' authors. • **Organize your ideas.** Present your ideas in a way that is coherent and shows a logical progression.
Conclusion: • Restate your thesis. • End with some final insights into your research. • Create a References list.	• **Return your readers to the purpose of your research.** Smoothly integrate into the conclusion a restatement of your thesis. Add any final insights. • **Provide an alphabetically arranged list with complete publication information for each source you used.** The list should appear on a separate page (or pages) at the end of your paper.

Developing Paragraphs

In a research report or paper, paragraphs are usually arranged with a larger structure in mind. This structure consists of three basic parts: an **introduction**, a **body**, and a **conclusion**.

WRITING THE INTRODUCTION

The introductory paragraph is your reader's first impression of your paper and its topic. Introductions often have a similar structure. The writer "warms up" to the topic by moving from general information to a more specific statement or main idea—often the thesis. Your introductory paragraph should do three things.

- Grab your reader's attention.

- Provide necessary background information.

- State the thesis.

Remember that an introduction should "hook," or grab, your readers' attention. Experienced writers have many techniques for writing introductions that effectively introduce the topic and make readers pay attention:

- **Open with your thesis and a brief indication of how it will be supported.** This is especially helpful when the material is complex or the topic is unfamiliar to the intended audience.

- **Start with an intriguing question and then provide background information that leads to a thesis statement.** The actual thesis can come at the end of the first paragraph or even at the beginning of the second paragraph.

- **Begin with a story that sets the context for your thesis.** Everyone enjoys a brief anecdote or story that helps personalize the topic.

- **Use an unusual fact, idea, or opinion to introduce your topic and thesis.** The element of surprise can enlighten, inform, and pique a reader's interest at the same time.

- **Open with a quotation.** For example you could use a quotation from an expert that supports your thesis, a statement of agreement with the expert, and then your thesis statement. This approach is especially helpful when the audience is likely to be hard to convince.

WRITING THE BODY

The body of a research paper develops the thesis statement. Each major point of the thesis is supported, or proven, in one or more paragraphs. In an effective body, paragraphs must have sufficient detail and work together to meet the characteristics listed on the following page.

- **The paragraph has unity.** Each paragraph should be a complete unit with a beginning, a middle, and an end. Although there are many ways to structure effective paragraphs, all are essentially several sentences that support one controlling idea. The controlling idea should be clearly stated in a separate sentence, commonly referred to as a topic sentence.

- **The paragraph is focused.** Each paragraph should contain only information that supports or proves the controlling idea.

- **The order of the sentences within the paragraph is effective.** There are several ways to structure a paragraph. The placement of the topic sentence in the paragraph can vary. Although many writers prefer to place the topic sentence at the beginning of a paragraph, effective paragraphs can also be written with the topic sentence at the end or in the middle of the paragraph.

- **The prevailing voice is the active voice**. Sentences are written in one of two voices, passive or active. In the active voice, the subject of the verb performs an action. The sentence "Psychologists research the factors that control behavior" is in the active voice. By contrast, in the passive voice, the subject of a sentence receives an action, instead of performing it. "The factors that control behavior are researched by psychologists" is a passive version of the example above. At times you will find it more appropriate to use the passive voice, but in general, the active voice is preferable.

The final step in refining your paragraphs is to create a smooth logical flow from one paragraph to the next by inserting transitional sentences, phrases, or words that connect what is about to be discussed with the information just presented. Examples of transitional expressions include *secondly*, *conversely*, *in summary*, *another reason*, *the next step*, and *another factor*.

WRITING THE CONCLUSION

The concluding paragraph of your paper should reinforce the main idea stated in your thesis, tie ideas together, and leave the reader with a sense of closure. Consider the following possibilities:

- **Restate your thesis.** To make sure your main point hits home, say it again in a different way.

- **Close with a question or challenge.** Invite your readers to come to the conclusion you expect them to reach after having read your paper.

- **End with a quotation.** Use an interesting quotation from an expert that sums up your main point in a striking way.

- **Connect your thesis to the reader's personal experience.** Relating your main idea to the reader's life will help make your ideas relevant to the reader.

Name _____ Class _____ Date _____

Writing Your Research Paper

Complete a graphic organizer like the one below and use it to help you
write your first draft. Use additional paper if necessary.

INTRODUCTION

How will you capture your readers' attention?
What background information will you need to provide for your readers?
How will you answer your research question in your thesis statement?

BODY

First main point:	Second main point:	Third main point:
Evidence:	Evidence:	Evidence:

CONCLUSION

How will you restate your thesis?
What closing thought will you leave your readers to think about?

Quoting and Crediting Sources

Giving credit to your sources is an essential part of writing a psychology research paper. Using direct quotations, data, ideas, and facts from experts adds credibility and variety to your paper. Use the guidelines below to give credit to your sources according to APA style.

TIPS FOR QUOTING YOUR SOURCES

Quotations should be reproduced word for word. Follow these suggestions to use quotations effectively in your paper:

- **Use an ellipsis (three spaced periods) to show where you have omitted sections from quoted material.**

  Steinberg states, "Abused individuals might stay with partners not only for reasons of finances or fear, but because they truly believe . . . that abuse is part of love" (Steinberg, 1996, p. 73).

- **Use square brackets to surround any letters or words you might need to add to a quotation to make the quotation's meaning clear.**

  Steinberg (1996) suggests that "The [love] stories we invent draw on elements from our experience of living in the world" (p. 62).

- **Incorporate short quotations with fewer than 40 words into your text.** Enclose the quotation within double quotation marks. Place other punctuation, such as periods and commas, within quotation marks when they are part of the quoted material.

  After interviewing many people, Sternberg (1996) concluded that "love is a story" and "the [love] stories we invent draw on elements from our experience of living in the world" (p. 62).

- **Set off quotations of 40 or more words as "blocks."** Start a block quotation on a new line, and indent the block about half an inch from the left margin. Do not use quotation marks to enclose block quotations.

  > Steinberg (1996) explains how we develop love stories:
  > The stories we invent draw on elements from our experience of living in the world—from the fairy stories we heard as young children, from the models of love relationships we observe around us in parents and relatives, from television and movies, from conversations with other people about their relationships and so on. (p. 62)

CREDITING SOURCES

Using someone else's words or ideas without giving proper credit—
intentionally or unintentionally—is called plagiarism. Not only is
plagiarism dishonest, it's considered intellectual stealing. Therefore, the
best policy is to be mindful of giving credit to direct quotations and
restatements of the original ideas of others.

Guidelines for Crediting Sources

The following guidelines will help you determine when to credit a source.

- Credit the source of each direct quotation.

- Credit the source of any data from studies, surveys, polls, and other
  sources of unique or little-known information.

- Credit any original theory, opinion, or conclusion that is not your own.
  Never present another person's ideas as your own, even if you are
  paraphrasing them.

- Do not credit facts or general knowledge—information that appears in
  standard reference works or several sources.

Reference Citations in Text

APA style requires authors to use an author-date method of citation. These
citations give readers just enough information to find the full source listing
on the *References* page. Use the examples in the chart below as a guide for
making reference citations in text.

Source Type	Basic Form and Content
One Work by One Author	Walker (2000) found patients with dementia In a recent study of dementia (Sims 2000)
One Work by Multiple Authors	*First text citation*: Cornett, Ramos, Anderson, and Prejean (2008) found *Subsequent text citations*: Cornett et al. (2008) found
Groups as Authors	*First text citation*: (National Institute of Mental Health [NIMH], 2005) *Subsequent text citations*: (NIMH, 2005)
No Author	the *World Almanac* (2006)
More than One Source in the Same Citation	Past research (Schaeffer & Shepardson, 2001, 2003) Past research (Miles, 2001, 2003, 2008, in press)
Specific Part of a Source	(Evler & Gierhart, 2005, p. 334) (Shar, 2008, chap. 4)
Personal Communication	D. E. Walker (personal communication, October 7, 2008)

Guidelines for Placement

In addition to the rules for the content and form of citations, there are also rules about placement. The APA provides the following guidelines for placing parenthetical citations:

- If the name of the author appears as part of the text, cite only the year of publication in parentheses and place the citation by the author's name.

- In cases where the author's name is not used, put the citation as close to the information it documents as possible. Include in parentheses both the name of the author and the year of publication.

- When a work has two authors, place the citation after the last author's name. Always cite both names every time the reference occurs in text.

Creating a Reference List

According to APA style, all psychology research papers should include a reference list at the end of the paper. The list documents all of the sources, print and nonprint, that you credit in your paper. The guidelines below will help you create a reference list according to APA style.

GUIDELINES FOR PREPARING THE REFERENCE LIST

1. **Center the heading *References* on a separate page.**

2. **Begin each entry on a separate line.** Position the first line of the entry even with the left margin, and indent all other lines five spaces. Double-space all entries.

3. **Alphabetize the sources by authors' last names.** If there is no author, alphabetize by title ignoring the words *A*, *An*, or *The* and using the first letter of the next word.

4. **List multiple entries by the same author or authors by the year of publication.** Start with the earliest publication.

AUTHORSHIP

Use the following sample entries, in APA style, as a reference for preparing your reference list.

Single Author
Author, A. A. (Year of copyright). Title of article. *Title of Periodical, Vol. #,* pp. XX–XX. Retrieved month day, year, from source.

Two Authors
Author, A. A. & Author, B. B. (Year of copyright). *Title of work.* Location: Publisher.

Three Authors
Author, A. A., Author, B. B. & Author, C. C. (Year of copyright). *Title of work.* Location: Publisher.

Four or More Authors
If there are more than six authors, list the first six as above and then use the term "et al.," which stands for "and others."

Author, A. A., Author, B. B., Author, C. C., Author, D. D., Author, E. E., Author, F. F., et al (Year of copyright). Title of article. *Title of Periodical, Vol. #,* pp. XX–XX.

GENERAL FORMS

The examples below show basic elements of the most common types of sources, in the order and style in which each would appear in an entry.

Journal and Magazine Articles

Author, A. A., Author, B. B. & Author, C. C. (Year of copyright). Title of article. *Title of Periodical, Vol. #,* pp. XX–XX.

Newspaper Article

Author, A. A., Author, B. B. & Author, C. C. (Year of copyright). Title of article. *Title of Periodical, Vol. #,* pp. XX–XX.

Books, Brochures, Reports, Annuals, Audiovisual Materials

Author, A. A. (Year of copyright). *Title of work.* Location: Publisher.

Edited Book

Editor, A. A. (Ed.). (Year of copyright). *Title of work.* Location: Publisher.

Selection in a Book

Author, A. A. (Year of copyright). Title of entry. In *Title of work* (Vol. #, pp. XX–XX). Location: Publisher.

Print Encyclopedia Entry

Author, A. A. (Year of copyright). Title of entry. In *Title of encyclopedia* (Vol. #, pp. XX–XX).

Online Journal Article

Author, A. A. (Year of copyright). Title of article. *Title of journal, Vol. #,* pp. XX–XX. Retrieved month day, year, from URL.

Online Document

Author, A. A., Author, B. B. & Author, C. C. (Year of copyright). *Title of work.* Retrieved month day, year, from URL.

Sound Recording

Writer, A. (Year of copyright). *Title of song* [Recorded by artist if different from writer]. On Title of album [Medium of recording: CD, record, cassette, etc.]. Location: Label (Recording date if different from copyright date).

Film or Movie

Producer, A. (Producer) & Director A. (Writer/Director). (Year of Copyright). *Title of Film or Video* [Motion Picture]. Country of Origin: Movie Studio.

Strategies for Evaluating and Revising

Revising your paper can transform average work into a superior research paper. Once you have addressed all of the points in your outline, set your draft aside. Taking a break from writing can give you a fresh perspective that will help you more easily spot problems in your paper. Work with a peer to look at content and organization first; then, focus on style. Use the strategies below and the worksheets that follow to evaluate your draft and revise it to improve its content, organization, and style.

Evaluate Your Draft	
Re-read	Re-read your draft carefully—not once, but several times—focusing on content, organization, and style.
Ask	Ask a peer to read the draft, point out weak or confusing parts, and make suggestions.
Revise Content and Organization	
Add	Add sensory or factual details, examples, and illustrations. Add sentences and paragraphs. Add words and phrases (such as *as a result*, *for example*, *first*, and *however*) to connect ideas.
Delete	Delete words, sentences, and paragraphs that stray from your composition's main idea. Eliminate wordiness and unnecessary repetition.
Replace	Replace weak support with stronger points, more convincing logical evidence, or details that are more vivid.
Rearrange	Rearrange sentences and paragraphs to find the clearest order of ideas. Use the cut-and-paste function of a word-processing program to experiment with various arrangements.
Elaborate	Elaborate and support each main point by providing specific details, facts, examples, illustrations, sensory images, figurative details, quotations, or anecdotes.
Revise Style	
Fine-tune	Check to make sure each word you have used is the one that most precisely communicates your idea.
Eliminate	Eliminate clichés and slang.
Vary	Vary sentence length and structure. Combine sentences to add variety or complexity.
Avoid	Avoid using the passive voice.

Checklist for Evaluating a Draft

Use the checklist below to evaluate your draft.

1. **Organization.** Check the general form of the paper.

___ a. All required elements are included.

___ b. Information is presented in a logical sequence.

___ c. The paper is within the assigned length range.

2. **Introduction.** Check the introductory paragraph.

___ a. It includes a thesis statement.

___ b. It specifies issues to be discussed.

___ c. It explains the point of view to be taken.

___ d. It is brief and to the point.

___ e. It provides the overall focus of the paper.

___ f. It captures the reader's attention.

3. **Construction.** Check the mechanics form of the paper.

___ a. Spelling is correct.

___ b. Grammar is correct.

___ c. Punctuation is correct.

___ d. Paragraphs follow a logical sequence.

___ e. Narrative is complete and precise (it does not ramble).

___ f. In-text source citations and reference list entries are presented in acceptable form.

___ g. Paper is neatly typed or handwritten.

4. **Writing Style.** Check the presentation of information.

___ a. Topic sentence clearly states each paragraph's main idea.

___ b. One new idea is introduced in each paragraph.

___ c. Transitions lead smoothly from one idea to the next.

___ d. Writing voice is active, not passive

___ e. Style is appropriate for the topic and intended audience.

5. **Content.** Check the content of the paper.

___ a. Adequate background information is provided.

___ b. Problems, issues, and circumstances upon which critical interpretations are based are fully described.

APA Writing Guide

Revising
Worksheet 7

Improve Your Research Paper

Use the rubric in this chart to help you improve your research paper.

Questions	Do This	Changes You Made
1. Does the introduction hook the reader's attention, provide sufficient background information, and clearly state the thesis?	___ **Circle** the hook. ___ **Underline** background information. ___ **Bracket** the thesis statement.	
2. Are main ideas and supporting details relevant to the thesis?	___ **Highlight** the main ideas. ___ **Number** supporting details for each.	
3. Is there a balance among direct quotations, paraphrases, and summaries?	___ **Star** sentences containing direct quotations. If more than one third of the sentences are starred, revise.	
4. Are sources cited when necessary? Are citations correctly placed and punctuated?	___ **Place check marks** by material from outside sources that requires documentation.	
5. Does the conclusion effectively restate the thesis and main idea of the paper?	___ **Bracket** the restatement of the thesis.	
6. Is the *Reference List* complete and correctly formatted?	___ **Place an X** beside *Reference List* entries of each source cited in the body of the paper.	

Peer and Self Evaluation Form

Use the following questions to evaluate your literary research paper or that of one of your classmates.

- Make brief notes to answer the questions.
- Rate the parts of the essay. The lowest score is **1**, and the highest is **4**.
- Make at least three suggestions for improving the paper.

1. Does the opening get the reader's attention? How complete is the background information?

   Rating: 1   2   3   4

   Suggestion: _____

2. Does the thesis identify the topic and main points? In the body of the report, how clearly do main ideas and supporting details relate to the thesis?

   Rating: 1   2   3   4

   Suggestion: _____

3. Are main points supported with details and evidence? Which main points could use more support?

   Rating: 1   2   3   4

   Suggestion: _____

4. Are all direct quotations, paraphrases, and summaries integrated into the paper and effective in supporting the main idea?

   Rating: 1   2   3   4

   Suggestion: _____

5. Is credit given for each source of information? Are the sources cited correctly?

   Rating: 1   2   3   4

   Suggestion: _____

6. How does the conclusion return the reader to the report's thesis?

   Rating: 1   2   3   4

   Suggestion: _____

Guidelines for Publishing

Publishing is the final stage in the writing process. In this stage, you prepare your paper for your actual readers. The guidelines below and worksheets that follow will help you prepare your paper for publication.

PROOFREAD YOUR DRAFT

Proofreading is essential to the publishing process. Mechanical errors—mistakes in capitalization, spelling, punctuation, grammar, and usage—distract readers and prevent them from paying attention to the strength of your ideas. Worksheet 9 will help you catch and correct mechanical errors.

   Learning and using standard proofreading symbols will help you correct your papers accurately and quickly. Worksheet 10 shows some common proofreading symbols. Worksheet 11 illustrates the use of proofreading symbols in an excerpt from a sample psychology paper. Use these symbols as you proofread your draft, and use them as a guide as you make your corrections and prepare your final copy.

PUBLISH YOUR PAPER

A published paper should have a clean, pleasant appearance and should not contain visual elements that distract the reader. Use the points below as a checklist for making sure that your paper looks its best.

- If handwritten, your letters are consistently and clearly formed, spacing is reasonable and uniform, and the words are easy to see and read.

- If typed, your text is in a font and size that is easy to read.

- There is a balance of white space (margins, the spaces between words and paragraphs) and text on the page that allows readers to focus on and easily read the text.

- Any titles, subheadings, page numbers, bullets, and other graphics are the appropriate size and boldness.

REFLECT ON YOUR COMPLETED PROJECT

Responding to the following questions will help you to think about what you have learned from this research project.

- What did I discover about my choice of topic? Did this topic hold my interest throughout the project? Why or why not?

- What additional research questions would I like to answer if I were to continue researching this topic?

- What mistakes did I make in my research procedures? How could I avoid making the same mistakes again?

- What did I enjoy about this project? Of what part am I proudest? Why?

Name _____ Class _____ Date _____

APA Writing Guide

Publishing
Worksheet 9

Proofreading Your Paper

Use the guidelines below to proofread and revise your paper.

Guidelines for Proofreading	Yes	No	Needs Work
Is every sentence in your paper complete—not a fragment or a run-on?			
Are punctuation marks—such as end marks, commas, semicolons, colons, dashes, and quotation marks—used correctly?			
Are proper nouns, proper adjectives, and the first words of sentences capitalized?			
Does every verb agree in number with its subject?			
Are verbs and tenses used correctly?			
Are subject and object forms of personal pronouns used correctly?			
Does every pronoun agree with its antecedent in number and in gender? Are pronoun references clear?			
Are frequently confused words (such as *fewer* and *less*, *affect* and *effect*) used correctly?			
Are all words spelled correctly? Are the plural forms of words correct?			
Is the paper neat and correct in form?			

APA Writing Guide

Publishing
Worksheet 10

Symbols for Proofreading and Editing

As you proofread and revise your draft, use the symbols below to indicate changes to correct in your final version.

Symbols for Editing and Proofreading		
Symbol	**Example**	**Meaning of Symbol**
cap /	Fifty-first street	Capitalize a lowercase letter.
lc /	Freud's Theory	Lowercase a capital letter.
∧	differant (e)	Change a letter.
∧	stages psychosocial development (of)	Insert a missing word, letter or punctuation mark.
∧	several reasons (factors)	Replace a word.
ℓ	Where's the the key?	Delete a word, letter, or punctuation mark.
⊺	a theory of inequality	Delete and close space.
⌒	a close friend ship	Close up space.
tr /	thier	Transpose, or change the order of the letters.
move /	Avoid having too many corrections of your paper in the final version	Move the circled words. (Write *move* in nearby margin.)
¶	¶Child abuse runs in families.	Begin a new paragraph.
⊙	Stay well⊙	Add a period.
⌄	Of course you may be wrong.	Add a comma.
#	mass consumption	Add a space.
⊙	one of the following⊙	Add a colon.
⋀	Maria Simmens, M.D. Jim Fiorello, PhD	Add a semicolon.
=	a great grand mother	Add a hyphen.
⌄	Pauls family history	Add an apostrophe.
stet /	On the fifteenth of July	Keep the crossed-out material. (Write *stet* in nearby margin.)

Proofreading Sample

Read aloud the text excerpt with one reader's corrections. Notice how distracting the errors are as you read. Then rewrite the paragraph on a separate sheet of paper, making all of the corrections.

Abraham Maslow organized human needs into a hierarchy—

a ranking of items in order of importance. at the bottom of the hier-   (cap)/

archy are biological ones. The need for self-actualization is at the   needs⊙/

top Maslow believed that once a person's needs are satisfied at   ⊙/

one level the person will try to satisfy needs at the next highest

level. For example, once food and drink have satisfied a person's   (tr)/

biological needs, that person will then means to satisfy safety   try (stet)/

needs, such as the needs for various kinds of shelter and security.

Maslow believed that people rise naturally through the levels of

this Hierarchy as long as they do not encounter overwhelming   (lc)/(#)/

obstacles along the way. Many people seek self-actualization

through work, hobbies and aesthetic experiences such as music,   ^⌃/

art, and poetry Critics of Maslow's hierarchy of needs argue that it   ¶/

does not apply to every one (Neher, 1991). For example, some

people show little interest in satisfying higher-level needs such as   ʒ/⌄⌃/

achievement and social recognition, even after their biological and

safety cancers have been met. But, one might ask, does their

apparent lack of interest stem from not having been motivated to

seek achievement or from having met with overwhelming obstacles ?   ^⌃/⌄/

Part 2: ASA Writing Guide

THE PREWRITING STAGE The prewriting stage is where you identify your purpose and audience, decide what to write about, draw upon what you know about the topic, and plan. The guidelines and worksheets that follow for setting goals and limits, choosing a topic, and gathering information will help you as you plan your paper.

Setting Goals and Limits

Before you begin a trip, you must know your destination—where you want to go. You must also consider the travel options that are available and the limits, such as time and money, you have for the trip. Likewise, before you begin the process of writing a paper, you must determine not only what you want the paper to achieve but what is possible given the assignment schedule and available resources. Set your goals and determine the limits of your paper by considering the points that follow.

- **Understand the final product.** Make sure that you understand the exact form and requirements of your research paper. How long should your paper be? Should it be typed or handwritten? What elements— title page, abstract, reference list, and so forth—must be included?

- **Create a project time line for your paper.** Count the days between the day you can begin working on the paper and the date it is due. Set up a time line that shows the date by which you will complete each stage of the writing process.

- **Determine the purpose of your paper.** The purpose of your paper will influence how you select, include, and present information. A paper can have more than one purpose—to inform and to persuade, for example. Other examples of purpose are to compare and contrast, to take a stand and defend it, and to explain or describe. Even though your main purpose is to inform, you may also have a secondary purpose—to compare and contrast, to explain a causal relationship, or to analyze data that you have collected. If the assignment does not specify the purpose of the paper, you must do so.

- **Identify your audience.** Who is your likely audience? If readers do not already know something about your topic, you will need to provide background information.

- **Think about how you will be evaluated.** Ask your teacher for a description of the criteria that will be used to evaluate your paper. List the criteria point by point. To the list, add the personal goals and standards that you want your paper to achieve. Use the final list to create an evaluation checklist that you can refer to as you develop your paper.

Choosing a Topic

Try to write about something that interests you. If you have been assigned a topic that holds little appeal for you, perhaps you can find an interesting aspect of it on which to concentrate.

Even if you have already chosen or been assigned a broad topic, you should take time to refine it to match your goals and suit your audience within the space and time limits of the assigned paper. Narrowing your topic before you begin will simplify and hasten the research process.

IDEAS AND CONTENT

- **Explore ideas and choose a topic.** Ask questions. Try finding a topic by asking questions about subjects that interest you.

- **Gather ideas and details to develop the topic.** Look at good sources of information, such as books, magazines, encyclopedias, the Internet, and experts in your community. Then provide logical support for your ideas by using facts, examples, statistics, and expert opinions.

- **Think about your audience and your purpose for writing.** Ask "Who am I writing for?" "What do my readers need to know?" "What will they find interesting?" "Why am I writing this paper?"

ORGANIZATION

- **Develop a thesis or controlling idea.** Narrow your topic so that it is not too big. For example, the topic of "the most influential sociological theories" is too big. An explanation of Émile Durkheim's definition of function is too narrow. You need something in between, such as how Durkheim's functionalist view of society influenced the field of sociology.

- **Organize the ideas and details into a coherent structure.** Try using order of importance. Start with your least important idea and save the most important idea for last. That way, the reader will better remember your most important ideas.

VOICE

- **Think about your topic—what voice should you use?** Your tone (friendly, calm, stern, neutral) should match your purpose and your topic. For example, a paper about the causes and effects of violence needs to be formal, and serious.

Choosing a Topic

Use the graphic organizer and questions below to help you choose a topic, plan research questions, and find sources.

- Choose and narrow a topic that can be researched and will provide information to your reader.

- Answer the questions below to help you organize your thoughts and begin your research.

CHOOSE AND NARROW A RESEARCH TOPIC

Broad topic	
Narrower topic	
Limited topic	

ANSWER QUESTIONS FOR RESEARCH

1. What do I already know about my topic? _____

_____

_____

2. What will my audience want to know about my topic? _____

_____

_____

3. What about my topic interests me? _____

_____

_____

4. What do I need to know about my topic? _____

_____

_____

Writing a Thesis Statement

A thesis statement is a sentence or two identifying the main idea that you intend to explain or prove in your paper. Taking the following steps will help you identify your thesis.

REFRESH YOUR MEMORY

Pick a topic. Then read through your notes and skim your resources to refresh your memory of the information you have.

ASK QUESTIONS

Think about what you now know about the topic. Ask yourself questions about the topic that might lead you to your thesis. Don't try too hard to think of questions appropriate for a paper at this point. Just let your mind explore the topic and allow questions to occur naturally.

EVALUATE YOUR QUESTIONS

Consider your questions one at a time for thesis potential. For example, suppose you were assigned the broad topic of "youth gangs." You might come up with the following questions:

- **Question A** Why are there so many causes and effects of gang violence?

- **Question B** Why do so many articles, songs, and movies focus on gang violence?

- **Question C** Is the rate of teen gang participation increasing?

- **Question D** Is there a link between drug and alcohol use and teen participation in gang violence?

- **Question E** What motivates teens from low-income areas of cities and towns to join gangs?

Because **Question A** is vague, it does not fit a sociology assignment very well. You may discard this question as a basis for your thesis statement.

At first glance, **Question B** seems unrelated to the assignment. As you think the question through, however, you realize that it implies a consumer demand for media about gang violence. A new question comes to mind—Is the rate of gang violence increasing? This question has thesis potential; you set it aside for now.

Several studies have concluded that the rate of gang violence has increased, so answering **Question C** may not provide new information. Still, evaluating your questions leads you to **Question D** and **Question E**, both of which have thesis potential. You now have three questions that might serve as the basis of your thesis. Choose the question that interests you most.

ANSWER YOUR QUESTION

Suppose you chose the following question: Why do teenagers from low-income areas of cities and towns to join gangs? Think of possible answers to your question, such as the following: Many teenagers in low-income areas have friends and family members who belong to gangs. These teenagers may join gangs to strengthen friendships and family ties. Others participate in gangs because they believe that the gang will protect them. Still, other young people join gangs to sell drugs and make money. Lastly, some teenagers believe that, if they refuse to join a gang, the gang might punish or harm them. Now identify relationships among your answers. For this set of answers you might identify the following points:

- Teenagers join gangs for social reasons.
- Teenagers join gangs for protection.
- Teenagers join gangs for financial reasons.
- Teenagers join gangs because they were forced or coerced to do so.

WRITE AND REFINE YOUR THESIS

Again, the thesis statement gives the main point of the paper. Consider the points you have come up with. Choose one or combine two or more of these points to formulate a rough thesis statement. For example: Teens join gangs for a variety of reasons.

To be effective, a thesis statement must meet the following criteria:

- answer a relevant question that could be asked about the topic,
- contain qualifiers that limit the statement to a precise and defensible point,
- be an affirmative statement, and
- be as brief as possible (one sentence is ideal).

Apply these criteria to the rough thesis statement above. The first criterion is met because the rough thesis statement would answer the question "Why do teenagers from low-income areas of cities and towns to join gangs?" The next criterion is not met because, as the statement now reads, it is vague and does not express a precise and defensible point.

You could refine the rough thesis statement to read: Understanding why teenagers in low-income areas join gangs can help sociologists plan effective gang prevention programs. Continuing with your evaluation, you see the thesis statement is now limited, is affirmative, and is brief. In short, it meets all of the remaining criteria. You may revise your thesis statement as you work on your paper, but for now, use what you settle on as your guide. Worksheet 2 provides practice in writing thesis statements.

Writing a Thesis Statement

Use the graphic organizer and questions below to write and refine a thesis statement based on your topic.

- Brainstorm a list of potential research questions about your topic and evaluate your questions for thesis potential.
- Select a research question to answer and write a thesis statement

ASK QUESTIONS ABOUT YOUR TOPIC

Questions	Thesis Potential
Question 1:	___ Yes ___ No
Question 2:	___ Yes ___ No
Question 3:	___ Yes ___ No
Question 4:	___ Yes ___ No
Question 5:	___ Yes ___ No

WRITE A THESIS STATEMENT

My research question:
Answer to my research question:
My thesis statement:

Gathering and Organizing Information

You will save yourself a great deal of time if you do some preliminary planning before beginning the information-gathering part of your research. You have already chosen a topic that arouses your curiosity, one about which you have questions. These questions can give your research some direction. You might want to brainstorm or use the *5W-How?* questions (who, what, when, where, why, and how) to help define your topic and clarify how best to proceed with research. For example, the questions below could help guide research on why young people join gangs.

- **Who** is most likely to join gangs?
- **What** can be done to prevent teenagers from joining gangs?
- **When** are young people most likely to engage in gang activity?
- **Where** are gangs most likely to operate?
- **Why** do many teenagers in low-income areas join gangs?
- **How** can sociologists help plan effective gang prevention programs?

FINDING SOURCES OF INFORMATION

Begin your research with a general look at, or overview, of your topic. Try one or a combination of the following sources to construct an overview. Not only will you find valuable background information, but you may also get leads on additional sources.

- In encyclopedias or other general reference books, read one or two articles about your topic, or if the topic is highly limited, about related topics. For example, you would not find an article explaining why people purchase products to improve their memory. You would, however, find articles on memory and memory loss, both of which are general topics.

- Search the Internet for information about your topic. Besides providing information you might use, a Web site might provide links to other useful sites.

- Interview an expert (a teacher, professor, librarian, parent, or neighbor) on your, topic. Such a person might be able to direct you to research materials that would prove extremely useful.

Once you have an adequate overview of your topic, you are ready to look for specific sources of information. All sources can be classified as either primary or secondary. A **primary source** provides firsthand, original information. It may be a letter, speech, research report, eyewitness account, personal remembrance, or autobiography. A **secondary source** contains secondhand, or indirect, information. An encyclopedia, an expert's opinion, a magazine article, and a biography are all secondary sources—

someone's interpretation, analysis, or opinion of primary sources. Because each type has its advantages, good researchers draw information from both sources. Primary sources present you with original material that you can interpret for yourself. Secondary sources present you with the perspectives of others who have studied your topic. Of course, in your search for information, you will want to explore both print and nonprint sources.

Sources of Information

Library Resources

Source	What to Look for
Card catalog or online catalog	Books, records, audiotapes, and videotapes (print and audiovisual listings are in separate catalogs in some libraries)
Online periodical indexes	Magazine and journal articles, indexed by subject and author
Indexes to newspapers, essays and articles	Articles from major newspapers, such as *The New York Times*; possible local newspapers (Newspapers are frequently archived online or on microfilm)
Specialized reference books and CD-ROMs	Encyclopedias of special subjects, such as almanacs and biographical references
Online databases, microfilm, or microfiche	Indexes to major newspapers; back issues of many major newspapers and magazines

Community Resources

Source	What to Look for
Internet and online services	Articles, interviews, bibliographies, pictures, videos, and sound recordings
Museums, historical societies, professional organizations, and government offices	Exhibits, records, and experts
Schools and colleges	Libraries, experts, exhibits, special collections, and records
Television and radio, videostores	Documentary and instructional programs and videos.

EVALUATE YOUR SOURCES

Because so many sources are available, you may have difficulty knowing which ones to use to evaluate the sources you find. Apply the *4R* test.

- **Relevant?** The source must contain information directly related to your topic.

- **Recent?** Always use sources that are as current as possible. Even in a slow-changing field of psychology, you should read the most recent publications. They will often show you, in their bibliographies, which older sources of information are still important.

- **Reliable?** The source must be accurate. Generally, a respected scholar or a respected newspaper or journal, such as *The Washington Post* or *Newsweek*, will provide trustworthy information. If in doubt about a source, consult a librarian or expert.

- **Representative?** If your topic is controversial, find sources with information and opinions supporting both sides, even if you draw a conclusion that one side's position is stronger.

ORGANIZE YOUR SOURCES

Just as you have consulted references cited in secondary works, readers of your research paper may want to consult your sources for additional information on your topic. In a References list at the end of your paper, you will need to provide precise details about every source you have used. For this reason, always carefully record information about sources as you use them. Otherwise, you may find yourself running back to the library or making a hasty, last-minute phone call to track down source information.

Use the suggestions below to help you record your sources. Completing Worksheet 3 will help you learn the correct style for noting sources.

- **Make a source card or bibliography card for every source you use.** You may keep your list on index cards, in a computer file, or simply on several pages of a notebook.

- **Number your sources. Assign each source a number.** Then you can write the number, rather than author and title, when you are taking notes from a given source.

- **Record all publishing information.** Take down everything you might need for your References list, such as title and subtitle, an editor or translator, volume number, city, publisher, original publication date, and revised edition date.

- **Note the call number or the location of the source.** This information will save you time if you must go back to a source later.

RESEARCH AND TAKE NOTES

Now you are ready to leap into a major phase of your research project—the search for specific information. As you examine your source material, you will take notes on the facts, examples, and opinions pertinent to your topic. There are three ways to record this information: **summarizing**, **paraphrasing**, and **quoting directly**.

Note-Taking Strategies	
Strategy	**Use**
A **summary** is a brief restatement of main ideas and important details.	To note general ideas about your topic that do not require detailed discussion, such as an alternative viewpoint
A **paraphrase** is a restatement that retains more details than a summary and is about the same length as the original.	To include pertinent details, such as names, dates, and statistics
A **direct quotation** is the exact words of an author or speaker and is always enclosed in quotation marks.	To note ideas that are especially well phrased, to be sure of technical accuracy, and to refer to passages from works of literature

CREATE NOTE CARDS

Use the guidelines below for creating note cards. Completing Worksheet 3 will help you learn the correct style for taking notes.

- **Use a separate note card, sheet of paper, or computer file for each source and for each main idea.** Having separate records for each source and each main idea will make sorting and grouping your notes easier.

- **Write the source number in the upper right-hand corner and the page number(s) at the bottom of the note card.** Both numbers are essential for correct documentation. The source number gives you access to the publication data on your corresponding source card. The page numbers must be supplied if you use the information in your paper.

- **Write a label at the top of the card showing the main idea.** The labels will let you see content at a glance and are useful in preparing your working outline.

- **Re-read the note to make sure you understand it.** Decipher any abbreviations or note-taking shortcuts that might be unclear when you are writing your paper.

Making Source Cards and Note Cards

Use graphic organizers like the ones below to record sources and take notes.

- Make a source card for each of your sources.
- Complete your note cards. Make sure to record quotes accurately, give credit to authors, and paraphrase by completely rewriting ideas.

SAMPLE SOURCE CARD

Source number: _____

Publishing information:

Annotation:

Call number:

SAMPLE NOTE CARD

Source number: _____

Heading (the main idea):

Note (direct quotation, paraphrase, or summary):

Page number: _____

THE WRITING STAGE In the writing stage you express your main ideas clearly, support those ideas, and follow a plan of organization, adjusting the plan as needed to make meaning clear. The guidelines that follow and Worksheet 4 will help you as you write your first draft.

Organizing Information

With your topic clearly defined and your thesis statement as a guide, you are now ready to organize the mass of information that you have collected. Every essay or paper has three parts: an introduction that usually states the thesis, a body that presents at least two supporting points, and a conclusion that summarizes and supports the main point.

If you have labeled notes by main idea, you can sort your notes into groups by main idea. You can set aside notes that aren't useful, and then arrange and rearrange the ones you plan to use until you have identified an organizational pattern for your paper. The chart below provides definitions and examples of some organizational patterns.

Types of Organizational Patterns in Writing		
Pattern	**When Writers Use It**	**How It Works**
Chronological	• to tell a story or relate an event or experience • to explain a process • to show cause and effect	• presents events in the order they occur • shows how things change over time
Spatial	• to describe individual features • to create a complete visual picture	• arranges details by location in space—for example, top to bottom, left to right, clockwise, or near to far
Order of Importance	• to inform • to persuade	• arranges ideas and details from most important to least or vice versa • places emphasis where writer thinks it is most effective
Logical	• to inform or to persuade, often by classifying: defining, dividing a subject into parts, or comparing and contrasting	• groups ideas or details together in ways that illustrate the relationships between them

MAPPING INFORMATION

Organizing your notes and identifying an organizational pattern for your paper paves the way for your outline. An **informal outline**, which allows you to organize main ideas and supporting details without arranging them into outline form with numbers and letters, may be all that you need. Strategies for creating informal outlines include **clustering** and **mapping**. The figure below shows an example of clustering.

Sample Cluster Map: Social Inequality

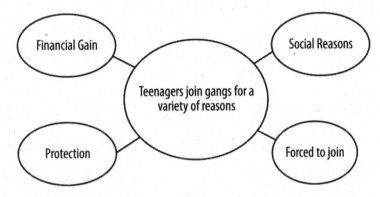

OUTLINING INFORMATION

Your teacher may also require that you turn in a final, formal outline to serve as a table of contents for your final paper. This outline must follow standard outline format as shown in the partial outline below. Completing **Worksheet 4** will help you organize your notes in outline form.

Sample Outline: Teenagers and Gang Membership

   I. Introduction

  II. Reasons for Joining Gangs

     A. Social Reasons

        1. Sense of Belonging

        2. Friends and Family Members

     B. Protection

     C. Financial Reasons

        1. Drugs

        2. Other Criminal Activity

     D. Forced to Join

 III. Research

     A. Current Statistics

     B. Gang Prevention Programs

 IV. Conclusion

Preparing an Outline

Complete the graphic organizer below, and use it to help you write your
first draft. Include a list of your sources. Use additional paper if necessary.

TOPIC: _____

OUTLINE
I. Introduction

A. Thesis statement:

_____

B. Background information:

_____

II. Body

A. First main point: _____

   1. Evidence: _____

      a. _____

      b. _____

   2. Evidence: _____

      a. _____

      b. _____

B. Second main point: _____

   1. Evidence: _____

      a. _____

      b. _____

   2. Evidence: _____

      a. _____

      b. _____

C. Third main point: _____

   1. Evidence: _____

      a. _____

      b. _____

   2. Evidence: _____

      a. _____

      b. _____

III. Conclusion

A. Restatement of thesis:

_____

B. Closing thought:

_____

SOURCES

1.
2.
3.
4.

Drafting the Paper

Before you begin writing, gather all of your notes, your outline, and any other materials. Then, use the framework for writing below along with the guidelines for developing paragraphs that follow and Worksheet 5 to write your first draft.

Writing a Research Paper	
Framework	**Directions and Explanations**
Introduction: • Hook your readers. • Provide necessary background. • Include your thesis statement.	• **Use a title page and formal outline if appropriate.** Follow your teacher's instructions. • **Grab your readers' attention right away.** Use a vivid scene, interesting detail, or striking quotation. • **Include background information.** Provide readers with enough background about your topic to make your paper understandable. • **State your thesis.** Clearly state your main idea about your research; incorporate it smoothly into the introduction.
Body: • Develop the first idea that supports your thesis. • Develop the second idea and so on.	• **Present your research.** Be certain that you support each major point about your thesis with evidence from a variety of sources. Be sure to cite your sources, and distinguish your own ideas from those of your sources' authors. • **Organize your ideas.** Present your ideas in a way that is coherent and shows a logical progression.
Conclusion: • Restate your thesis. • End with some final insights into your research. • Create a References list.	• **Return your readers to the purpose of your research.** Smoothly integrate into the conclusion a restatement of your thesis. Add any final insights. • **Provide an alphabetically arranged list with complete publication information for each source you used.** The list should appear on a separate page (or pages) at the end of your paper.

Developing Paragraphs

In a research report or paper, paragraphs are usually arranged with a larger structure in mind. This structure consists of three basic parts: an **introduction**, a **body**, and a **conclusion**.

WRITING THE INTRODUCTION

The introductory paragraph is your reader's first impression of your paper and its topic. Introductions often have a similar structure. The writer "warms up" to the topic by moving from general information to a more specific statement or main idea—often the thesis. Your introductory paragraph should do three things.

- Grab your reader's attention.
- Provide necessary background information.
- State the thesis.

Remember that an introduction should "hook," or grab, your readers' attention. Experienced writers have many techniques for writing introductions that effectively introduce the topic and make readers pay attention:

- **Open with your thesis and a brief indication of how it will be supported.** This is especially helpful when the material is complex or the topic is unfamiliar to the intended audience.

- **Start with an intriguing question and then provide background information that leads to a thesis statement.** The actual thesis can come at the end of the first paragraph or even at the beginning of the second paragraph.

- **Begin with a story that sets the context for your thesis.** Everyone enjoys a brief anecdote or story that helps personalize the topic.

- **Use an unusual fact, idea, or opinion to introduce your topic and thesis.** The element of surprise can enlighten, inform, and pique a reader's interest at the same time.

- **Open with a quotation.** For example you could use a quotation from an expert that supports your thesis, a statement of agreement with the expert, and then your thesis statement. This approach is especially helpful when the audience is likely to be hard to convince.

WRITING THE BODY

The body of a research paper develops the thesis statement. Each major point of the thesis is supported, or proven, in one or more paragraphs. In an effective body, paragraphs must have sufficient detail and work together to meet the characteristics listed on the following page.

- **The paragraph has unity.** Each paragraph should be a complete unit with a beginning, a middle, and an end. Although there are many ways to structure effective paragraphs, all are essentially several sentences that support one controlling idea. The controlling idea should be clearly stated in a separate sentence, commonly referred to as a topic sentence.

- **The paragraph is focused.** Each paragraph should contain only information that supports or proves the controlling idea.

- **The order of the sentences within the paragraph is effective.** There are several ways to structure a paragraph. The placement of the topic sentence in the paragraph can vary. Although many writers prefer to place the topic sentence at the beginning of a paragraph, effective paragraphs can also be written with the topic sentence at the end or in the middle of the paragraph.

- **The prevailing voice is the active voice.** Sentences are written in one of two voices, passive or active. In the active voice, the subject of the verb performs an action. The sentence "Sociologists research the social factors that influence behavior" is in the active voice. By contrast, in the passive voice, the subject of a sentence receives an action, instead of performing it. "The social factors that influence behavior are researched by sociologists" is a passive version of the example above. At times you will find it more appropriate to use the passive voice, but in general, the active voice is preferable.

The final step in refining your paragraphs is to create a smooth logical flow from one paragraph to the next by inserting transitional sentences, phrases, or words that connect what is about to be discussed with the information just presented. Examples of transitional expressions include *secondly*, *conversely*, *in summary*, *another reason*, *the next step*, and *another factor*.

WRITING THE CONCLUSION

The concluding paragraph of your paper should reinforce the main idea stated in your thesis, tie ideas together, and leave the reader with a sense of closure. Consider the following possibilities:

- **Restate your thesis.** To make sure your main point hits home, say it again in a different way.

- **Close with a question or challenge.** Invite your readers to come to the conclusion you expect them to reach after having read your paper.

- **End with a quotation.** Use an interesting quotation from an expert that sums up your main point in a striking way.

- **Connect your thesis to the reader's personal experience.** Relating your main idea to the reader's life will help make your ideas relevant to the reader.

ASA Writing Guide

Writing
Worksheet 5

Writing Your Research Paper

Complete a graphic organizer like the one below and use it to help you write your first draft. Use additional paper if necessary.

INTRODUCTION

How will you capture your readers' attention?
What background information will you need to provide for your readers?
How will you answer your research question in your thesis statement?

BODY

First main point:	Second main point:	Third main point:
Evidence:	Evidence:	Evidence:

CONCLUSION

How will you restate your thesis?
What closing thought will you leave your readers to think about?

Quoting and Crediting Sources

Giving credit to your sources is an essential part of writing a psychology research paper. Using direct quotations, data, ideas, and facts from experts adds credibility and variety to your paper. Use the guidelines below to give credit to your sources according to ASA style.

TIPS FOR QUOTING YOUR SOURCES

Quotations should be reproduced word for word. Follow these suggestions to use quotations effectively in your paper:

- **Use an ellipsis (three spaced periods) to show where you have omitted sections from quoted material.**

  Steinberg states, "Abused individuals might stay with partners not only for reasons of finances or fear, but because they truly believe . . . that abuse is part of love" (Steinberg 1996: P. 73).

- **Use square brackets to surround any letters or words you might need to add to a quotation to make the quotation's meaning clear.**

  Steinberg (1996) suggests that "The [love] stories we invent draw on elements from our experience of living in the world" (P. 62).

- **Incorporate short quotations with fewer than 40 words into your text.** Enclose the quotation within double quotation marks. Place other punctuation, such as periods and commas, within quotation marks when they are part of the quoted material.

  After interviewing many people, Sternberg (1996) concluded that "love is a story" and "the [love] stories we invent draw on elements from our experience of living in the world" (P. 62).

- **Set off quotations of 40 or more words as "blocks."** Start a block quotation on a new line, and indent the block about half an inch from the left margin. Do not use quotation marks to enclose block quotations.

  Steinberg (1996) explains how we develop love stories:

  > The stories we invent draw on elements from our experience of living in the world—from the fairy stories we heard as young children, from the models of love relationships we observe around us in parents and relatives, from television and movies, from conversations with other people about their relationships and so on. (p. 62)

CREDITING SOURCES

Using someone else's words or ideas without giving proper credit—
intentionally or unintentionally—is called plagiarism. Not only is
plagiarism dishonest, it's considered intellectual stealing. Therefore, the
best policy is to be mindful of giving credit to direct quotations and
restatements of the original ideas of others.

Guidelines for Crediting Sources

The following guidelines will help you determine when to credit a source.

- Credit the source of each direct quotation.

- Credit the source of any data from studies, surveys, polls, and other
  sources of unique or little-known information.

- Credit any original theory, opinion, or conclusion that is not your own.
  Never present another person's ideas as your own, even if you are
  paraphrasing them.

- Do not credit facts or general knowledge—information that appears in
  standard reference works or several sources.

Reference Citations in Text

ASA style requires authors to use an author-date method of citation. These
citations give readers just enough information to find the full source listing
on the *References* page. Use the examples in the chart below as a guide for
making reference citations in text.

Source Type	Basic Form and Content
One Work by One Author	Walker (2000) found patients with dementia In a recent study of dementia (Walker 2000)
One Work by Three Authors	*First text citation*: In a report on drug use (Cornett, Ramos, and Prejean 2008) *Subsequent text citations*: Contrary to previous findings (Cornett et al. 2008)
One Work by More than Three Authors	*First text citation*: A new study (Sims et al. 2007) *Subsequent text citations*: New information (Sims et al. 2007)
Unpublished Materials	*Use* forthcoming *to indicate unpublished materials*: In a new study Marcus (forthcoming)
Sources with No Date	*Use* N.d. *to indicate sources with no date*: In a previous study Marcus (N.d.)
More than One Source in the Same Citation	*Use semicolons to separate a series of sources*: Past research (Schaeffer 1995; Shepardson 2001, 2003)
Specific Passage of a Source	(Evler and Gierhart, 2005: P. 334)

Guidelines for Placement

In addition to the rules for the content and form of citations, there are also rules about placement. The APA provides the following guidelines for placing parenthetical citations:

- If the name of the author appears as part of the text, cite only the year of publication in parentheses and place the citation by the author's name.

- In cases where the author's name is not used, put the citation as close to the information it documents as possible. Include in parentheses both the name of the author and the year of publication.

- When a work has two authors, place the citation after the last author's name. Always cite both names every time the reference occurs in text.

Creating a Reference List

According to ASA style, all psychology research papers should include a
reference list at the end of the paper. The list documents all of the sources,
print and nonprint, that you credit in your paper. The guidelines below will
help you create a reference list according to ASA style.

GUIDELINES FOR PREPARING THE REFERENCE LIST

1. **Center the heading *References* on a separate page.**

2. **Begin each entry on a separate line.** Position the first line of the entry even with
   the left margin, and indent all other lines five spaces. Double-space all entries.

3. **Alphabetize the sources by authors' last names.** If there is no author, alphabetize
   by title ignoring the words *A*, *An*, or *The* and using the first letter of the next word.

4. **List multiple entries by the same author or authors by the Year of Publication.**
   Start with the earliest publication.

AUTHORSHIP

For sources with multiple authors, invert only the first author's name, for
example: Cornett, Jarred and Shelley Harris. Use the following sample
entries, in ASA style, as a reference for preparing your reference list.

Single Author
Author, A. A. (Year of Publication). *Name of Publication*. Location of Publisher:
　　Publisher's Name.

Two Authors
Author, A. A. and B. B. Author, (Year of Publication). *Name of Publication*. Location of
　　Publisher: Publisher's Name.

Three Authors
Author, A. A., B. B. Author, and C. C. Author (Year of Publication). *Name of
　　Publication*. Location of Publisher: Publisher's Name.

GENERAL FORMS

The examples below show basic elements of the most common types of sources, in the order and style in which each would appear in an entry.

Journal and Magazine Articles

Author, A. A., B. B. Author and C. C. Author (Year of Publication). "Title of article." *Name of Publication* Volume Number (Issue Number): page numbers of article.

Newspaper Article

Author, A. A. and B. B. Author (Year of Publication). "Title of article." *Name of Publication* Volume Number (Issue Number): page numbers of article.

Books, Brochures, Reports, Annuals, Audiovisual Materials

Author, A. A. (Year of Publication). *Name of Publication*. Location of Publisher: Publisher's Name.

Sources with No Publication Date

Author, A. A. (N.d.). *Name of Publication*. Location of Publisher: Publisher's Name.

Edited Book

Editor, A. A. (Ed.). (Year of Publication). *Name of Publication*. Location of Publisher: Publisher's Name.

Selection in a Book

Author, A. A. (Year of Publication). "Title of entry." Pp. XX–XX in *Name of Publication*, edited by A. A. Editor. Location of Publisher: Publisher's Name.

Selection in a Book with Multiple Editors

Author, A. A. (Year of Publication). "Title of entry." Pp. XX–XX in *Name of Publication*, edited by A. A. Editor, B. B. Editor, and C. C. Editor. Location of Publisher: Publisher's Name.

Online Journal Article

Author, A. A. and B. B. Author (Year of Publication). "Title of article." *Name of Publication* Volume Number (Issue Number). Retrieved month day, year (URL).

Strategies for Evaluating and Revising

Revising your paper can transform average work into a superior research paper. Once you have addressed all of the points in your outline, set your draft aside. Taking a break from writing can give you a fresh perspective that will help you more easily spot problems in your paper. Work with a peer to look at content and organization first; then, focus on style. Use the strategies below and the worksheets that follow to evaluate your draft and revise it to improve its content, organization, and style.

Evaluate Your Draft	
Re-read	Re-read your draft carefully—not once, but several times—focusing on content, organization, and style.
Ask	Ask a peer to read the draft, point out weak or confusing parts, and make suggestions.
Revise Content and Organization	
Add	Add sensory or factual details, examples, and illustrations. Add sentences and paragraphs. Add words and phrases (such *as a result, for example, first*, and *however*) to connect ideas.
Delete	Delete words, sentences, and paragraphs that stray from your composition's main idea. Eliminate wordiness and unnecessary repetition.
Replace	Replace weak support with stronger points, more convincing logical evidence, or details that are more vivid.
Rearrange	Rearrange sentences and paragraphs to find the clearest order of ideas. Use the cut-and-paste function of a word-processing program to experiment with various arrangements.
Elaborate	Elaborate and support each main point by providing specific details, facts, examples, illustrations, sensory images, figurative details, quotations, or anecdotes.
Revise Style	
Fine-tune	Check to make sure each word you have used is the one that most precisely communicates your idea.
Eliminate	Eliminate clichés and slang.
Vary	Vary sentence length and structure. Combine sentences to add variety or complexity.
Avoid	Avoid using the passive voice.

Checklist for Evaluating a Draft

Use the checklist below to evaluate your draft.

1. **Organization.** Check the general form of the paper.

___ a. All required elements are included.

___ b. Information is presented in a logical sequence.

___ c. The paper is within the assigned length range.

2. **Introduction.** Check the introductory paragraph.

___ a. It includes a thesis statement.

___ b. It specifies issues to be discussed.

___ c. It explains the point of view to be taken.

___ d. It is brief and to the point.

___ e. It provides the overall focus of the paper.

___ f. It captures the reader's attention.

3. **Construction.** Check the mechanics form of the paper.

___ a. Spelling is correct.

___ b. Grammar is correct

___ c. Punctuation is correct.

___ d. Paragraphs follow a logical sequence.

___ e. Narrative is complete and precise (it does not ramble).

___ f. In-text source citations and reference list entries are presented in acceptable form.

___ g. Paper is neatly typed or handwritten.

4. **Writing Style.** Check the presentation of information.

___ a. Topic sentence clearly states each paragraph's main idea.

___ b. One new idea is introduced in each paragraph.

___ c. Transitions lead smoothly from one idea to the next.

___ d. Writing voice is active, not passive

___ e. Style is appropriate for the topic a.nd intended audience.

5. **Content.** Check the content of the paper.

___ a. Adequate background information is provided.

___ b. Problems, issues, and circumstances upon which critical interpretations are based are fully described.

Improve Your Research Paper

Use the rubric in this chart to help you improve your research paper.

Questions	Do This	Changes You Made
1. Does the introduction hook the reader's attention, provide sufficient background information, and clearly state the thesis?	___ **Circle** the hook. ___ **Underline** background information. ___ **Bracket** the thesis statement.	
2. Are main ideas and supporting details relevant to the thesis?	___ **Highlight** the main ideas. ___ **Number** supporting details for each.	
3. Is there a balance among direct quotations, paraphrases, and summaries?	___ **Star** sentences containing direct quotations. If more than one third of the sentences are starred, revise.	
4. Are sources cited when necessary? Are citations correctly placed and punctuated?	___ **Place check marks** by material from outside sources that requires documentation.	
5. Does the conclusion effectively restate the thesis and main idea of the paper?	___ **Bracket** the restatement of the thesis.	
6. Is the *Reference List* complete and correctly formatted?	___ **Place an X** beside *Reference List* entries of each source cited in the body of the paper.	

Peer and Self Evaluation Form

Use the following questions to evaluate your literary research paper or that of one of your classmates.

- Make brief notes to answer the questions.
- Rate the parts of the essay. The lowest score is **1**, and the highest is **4**.
- Make at least three suggestions for improving the paper.

1. Does the opening get the reader's attention? How complete is the background information?

   Rating: 1 2 3 4

   Suggestion: _____

2. Does the thesis identify the topic and main points? In the body of the report, how clearly do main ideas and supporting details relate to the thesis?

   Rating: 1 2 3 4

   Suggestion: _____

3. Are main points supported with details and evidence? Which main points could use more support?

   Rating: 1 2 3 4

   Suggestion: _____

4. Are all direct quotations, paraphrases, and summaries integrated into the paper and effective in supporting the main idea?

   Rating: 1 2 3 4

   Suggestion: _____

5. Is credit given for each source of information? Are the sources cited correctly?

   Rating: 1 2 3 4

   Suggestion: _____

6. How does the conclusion return the reader to the report's thesis?

   Rating: 1 2 3 4

   Suggestion: _____

Guidelines for Publishing

Publishing is the final stage in the writing process. In this stage, you prepare your paper for your actual readers. The guidelines below and worksheets that follow will help you prepare your paper for publication.

PROOFREAD YOUR DRAFT

Proofreading is essential to the publishing process. Mechanical errors—mistakes in capitalization, spelling, punctuation, grammar, and usage—will distract readers and prevent them from paying attention to the strength of your ideas. Worksheet 9 will help you catch and correct mechanical errors.

   Learning and using standard proofreading symbols will help you correct your papers accurately and quickly. Worksheet 10 shows some common proofreading symbols. Worksheet 11 illustrates the use of proofreading symbols in an excerpt from sample sociology paper. Use these symbols as you proofread your draft, and use them as a guide as you make your corrections and prepare your final copy.

PUBLISH YOUR PAPER

A published paper should have a clean, pleasant appearance and should not contain visual elements that may distract the reader. Use the points below as a checklist for making sure that your paper looks its best.

- If handwritten, your letters are consistently and clearly formed, spacing is reasonable and uniform, and the words are easy to see and read.

- If typed, your text is in a font and size that is easy to read.

- There is a balance of white space (margins, spaces between words and paragraphs) and text on the page that allows readers to focus on the text.

- Any titles, subheadings, page numbers, bullets, and other graphics are the appropriate size and boldness.

REFLECT ON YOUR COMPLETED PROJECT

Responding to the following questions will help you to think about what you have learned from this research project.

- What did I discover about my choice of topic? Did this topic hold my interest throughout the project? Why or why not?

- What additional research questions would I like to answer if I were to continue researching this topic?

- What mistakes did I make in my research procedures? How could I avoid making the same mistakes again?

- What did I enjoy about this project? Of what part am I proudest? Why?

Proofreading Your Paper

Use the guidelines below to proofread and revise your paper.

Guidelines for Proofreading	Yes	No	Needs Work
Is every sentence in your paper complete—not a fragment or a run-on?			
Are punctuation marks—such as end marks, commas, semicolons, colons, dashes, and quotation marks—used correctly?			
Are proper nouns, proper adjectives, and the first words of sentences capitalized?			
Does every verb agree in number with its subject?			
Are verbs and tenses used correctly?			
Are subject and object forms of personal pronouns used correctly?			
Does every pronoun agree with its antecedent in number and in gender? Are pronoun references clear?			
Are frequently confused words (such as *fewer* and *less*, *affect* and *effect*) used correctly?			
Are all words spelled correctly? Are the plural forms of words correct?			
Is the paper neat and correct in form?			

Name _____ Class _____ Date _____

Symbols for Proofreading and Editing

As you proofread and revise your draft, use the symbols below to indicate changes to correct in your final version.

Symbol	Example	Meaning of Symbol
	Symbols for Editing and Proofreading	
cap/	Fifty-first street	Capitalize a lowercase letter.
lc/	Freud's Theory	Lowercase a capital letter.
∧	differant (e)	Change a letter.
∧	stages (of) psychosocial development	Insert a missing word, letter or punctuation mark.
∧	several reasons (factors)	Replace a word.
ℐ	Where's the the key?	Delete a word, letter, or punctuation mark.
ℐ	a theory of inequality	Delete and close space.
⌒	a close friend ship	Close up space.
tr/	thier	Transpose, or change the order of the letters.
move/	Avoid having too many corrections of your paper in the final version	Move the circled words. (Write *move* in nearby margin.)
¶	¶ Child abuse runs in families.	Begin a new paragraph.
⊙	Stay well	Add a period.
⌒,	Of course you may be wrong.	Add a comma.
#	mass consumption	Add a space.
⊙:	one of the following	Add a colon.
⌃,	Maria Simmens, M.D. Jim Fiorello, PhD	Add a semicolon.
=	a great grand mother	Add a hyphen.
∨	Pauls family history	Add an apostrophe.
stet/	On the fifteenth of July	Keep the crossed-out material. (Write *stet* in nearby margin.)

ASA Writing Guide

Publishing

Proofreading Sample

Read aloud the text excerpt with one reader's corrections. Notice how distracting the errors are as you read. Then rewrite the paragraph on a separate sheet of paper, making all of the corrections.

Sociolinguist Deborah tannen has studied how men   (cap)/

and women communicate differently and how these

differences affect their interactions. According to Tannen,

boys and girls are essentially raised in different cultures,   (tr)/

which makes interaction between genders an exercise in   (stet)/

cross-cultural communication. Tannen argues that people

speak differently to boys and girls, even within the same

family. She also states that "children learn how to talk, how   ⌄⊙/

to have to have conversations, not only from their parents

but also from their peers." Anthropological studies show that   (#)/(¶)/

children spend most of their day playing in same-sex   time/

groups. Boys tend to play in large groups based on a

hierarchy with a Dominant leader. Boys are typically   (lc)/

encouraged to be competitive. In contrast girls often play in   ⌄⌃/

pairs or small groups. A best friend is at the center of a girl's

social life. Girls are typically encouraged to be cooperative.   ⌄⌄/

Tannen concludes that how children play influences how

they communicate both as children and as adults.   ⌄/

Some commonly used words and phrases make writing unnecessarily complicated. Use "plain" language to say only what needs to be said. This will enhance the readability of your writing. The following list presents common wordy phrases and suggests alternative expressions.

Wordy	Better
a considerable amount of	much
a considerable number of	many
a great deal of	much
a great majority of	most
a number of	a few, several, many, some
absolutely essential	essential
accounted for by	because, due to, caused by
add the point that	add that
adjacent to	near
along the lines of	like
an example of this is the fact that	for example
an order of magnitude faster	10 times faster
analyzation	analysis
another aspect of the situation	as for
are of the opinion that	think that, believe
are of the same opinion	agree
as a matter of fact	in fact
as in the case	as happens
as of this date	today
as per	[omit]
as regards	about
as related	for, about
as to	about
at a rapid rate	rapidly
at an earlier date	previously
at some future time	later
at the conclusion of	after
at the present time	now
at this point in time	now
based on the fact that	because
by means of	by, with
causal factor	cause
collect together	collect
completely full	full
concerning, concerning the nature of	about
consensus of opinion	consensus
considerable amount of	much
definitely proved	proved
demonstrate	show, prove
despite the fact that	although
due to the fact that	because, since

APA and ASA Writing Guide

Wordy	Better
during the course of	during, while
during the time that	while
enclosed herewith	enclosed
end result	result
endeavor	try
entirely eliminate	eliminate
eventuate	happen
except in small number of cases	usually
exhibit a tendency to	tend to
fatal outcome	death
few [many] in number	few [many]
fewer in number	fewer
finalize	end
first of all	first
firstly [secondly, etc.]	first [second, etc.]
for the purpose of	for, to
for the reasons that	because, since
from the point of view of	for
future plans	plans
give an account of	describe
give rise to	cause
has been engaged in a study of	has studied
has the capability of	can
have an input in	contribute to
have in regard to	about
have the appearance of	look like
if at all possible	if possible
impact [verb]	affect
important essentials	essentials
in a number of cases	some
in a position to	can, may
in a satisfactory manner	satisfactorily
in a very real sense	in a sense [or omit]
in almost all instances	nearly always
in case, in case of	if
in close proximity	close, near
in connection with	about, concerning
in favor of	for, to
in light of the fact that	because
in many cases	often
in my opinion it is not an unjustifiable assumption that	I think

Electronic Resources Glossary

The list below includes preferred spelling and definitions for some key terms used for electronic resources. This list is drawn from the *ASA Style Guide, The American Heritage Dictionary* (Fourth Edition), the *Chicago Manual of Style*, as well as from other sources.

Blog (n.) A term commonly used for a Web log, a personal journal that is published as a Web page and openly accessible to the public. Typically, authors update their blogs daily and design them to reflect their personalities. (v.) To author a Web log. Other forms: Blogger (a person who blogs). Retrieved January 15, 2007. (http://www.webopedia.com)

Database A collection of electronic data that has been organized by a computer program in such a way that the data can be easily and quickly searched, arranged, and retrieved. Also called a data bank.

Digital (adj.) Transmitted or stored in an electronic format; (n.) Of or relating to a device that can read, write, or store information that is represented in numerical form.

Disk A direct storage device for electronic data, such as a floppy disk, a hard disk, or a compact disk.

DVD *Digital Video Disc.* A high-density compact disk for storing large amounts of data, especially high-resolution audio-visual material.

Dpi *Dots per inch.* A measurement of the resolution of a printed image. The term is also used to describe the maximum resolution of the output device.

E-commerce Commerce that is transacted electronically, as over the Internet.

E-mail Electronic mail. (n.) A system for sending and receiving messages electronically over a computer network, as between personal computers; a message or messages sent or received by such a system. (v.) To send (a message) by such a system.

File A collection of related data or program records that is given a single name and that is stored as a unit in a specific location on a computer or on an external storage device. Examples of data stored in files include programs, text documents, and images.

FTP *File transfer protocol.* (n.) A communications protocol governing the transfer of files from one computer to another over a network. (v.) To transfer a file using FTP.

Homepage The opening or main page of a Web site, intended chiefly to greet visitors and provide information about the site or its owner.

Host A computer containing data or programs that another computer can access from a remote location by means of a network or modem.

HTML, html, .html *Hyper Text Markup Language.* A markup language that consists of a set of tags that are used to structure the text and multimedia documents on a Web page, and that set up hypertext links between different Web pages.

APA and ASA Writing Guide

Hypertext A computer-based text retrieval system that enables a user to access particular locations in pages or other electronic documents by clicking on links within specific Web pages or documents.

Internet A public network of computers that connects many smaller networks around the world.

LISTSERV A trademarked proprietary name that has been widely used to mean "electronic mailing list." The term LISTSERV should only be used to refer to the trademarked version.

Online Connected to a computer, computer network, or telecommunications network; accessible via a computer or computer network: *an online database.*

PDF, pdf, .pdf *Portable Document Format.* An Adobe™ file format that allows some editing, compresses the amount of memory needed for graphics, and is more uniform, causing fewer problems at the printer.

Protocol A standard procedure for regulating data transmission between computers.

Resolution The fineness of detail that can be distinguished in an image, as on a video display terminal.

Scan (v.) To search (stored data) automatically for specific data; to create a digital file of a text document or an image. (n.) A picture or an image produced by this means.

Search engine A software program that searches a database and gathers and reports information that contains or is related to specified terms; or a Web site whose primary function is providing a search engine for gathering and reporting information available on the Internet or a portion of the Internet.

Text file An informal term for a computer file that contains text, or content made up of alphanumeric characters.

URL (n.) *Uniform Resource Locator.* An Internet address (for example, http://www.hmhco.com), usually consisting of the access protocol (http), the domain name (www.hmhco.com), and optionally the path to a file or resource residing on that server.

Web page A document on the World Wide Web, consisting of an HTML file and any related files for scripts and graphics, and often hyperlinked to other documents on the Web.

Web site A set of interconnected Web pages, usually including a homepage, generally located on the same server, and prepared and maintained as a collection of information by a person, group, or organization.

World Wide Web (n.) abbr. WWW. The complete set of documents residing on all Internet servers that use the HTTP protocol, accessible to users via a simple point-and-click system.